# CONFESSING
# THE FAITH

*Study Guide*

# CONFESSING THE FAITH

*Study Guide*

Emily Van Dixhoorn

THE BANNER OF TRUTH TRUST

# THE BANNER OF TRUTH TRUST

*Head Office*
3 Murrayfield Road
Edinburgh
EH12 6EL
UK

*North America Sales*
PO Box 621
Carlisle
PA 17013
USA

banneroftruth.org

© The Banner of Truth Trust 2017

Reprinted 2018

\*

ISBN
Print: 978 1 84871 761 9
EPUB: 978 1 84871 762 6
Kindle: 978 1 84871 764 0

\*

Typeset in 10.5/13.5 Adobe Garamond Pro
at The Banner of Truth Trust, Edinburgh

Printed in the USA by
Versa Press Inc.,
East Peoria, IL.

# CONTENTS

# INTRODUCTION

WHY study man's word when you could be studying God's Word? Or to put the question differently, why study a confession about the Bible when you could study the Bible itself? Because confessions contain excellent summaries of biblical doctrine, and according to the Bible, doctrine matters—a lot! Paul commands Timothy 'Watch your life and doctrine closely. Persevere in them, because if you do, you will save both yourself and your hearers' (1 Tim. 4:16). Paul's command to Timothy holds for us too.

Even if we know we should study doctrine, this doesn't mean we will. Sometimes we need the encouragement of others to get the job done, or even to get started. I didn't read the Bible (the most important of all books) or study its doctrine until a friend invited me to join a group. Perhaps for some of you, the first time you'll study Christian doctrine will be with a group.

This study guide aims to make group study easy. The questions stick closely to the text of *Confessing the Faith* and follow the chapter subheadings that you will find there. Some questions cover essential doctrines; others track nuanced arguments; still others promote personal application. Each chapter ends with a consideration for prayer.

Many of us face overwhelming responsibilities already. Taking on another study can be daunting. Hopefully this tool will help you to jump right into doctrinal study and discussion. So let's not delay: gather a few friends, some church members, classmates, students, fellow teachers or family members and let's enjoy studying together!

### Acknowledgements

Just as I study in groups, I work in groups, and so I owe thanks to many people: to my daughter Victoria for discussing *Confessing the Faith* with me while it was still a manuscript; to Lynn Snuggs, Susan Yang, Elizabeth Flanagan, and Lucy Green who drafted questions; to my mother-in-law Thea Van Dixhoorn for typing up my notes and using it with a group in Canada; to the women at Grace Presbyterian Church in Vienna, Virginia who gave the study a test-drive and for the elders who supported us. I'm also thankful for pastors who have shown interest in this study guide and who have offered suggestions. Special thanks go to Rev. Jimmy Choi for editing several chapters and helping to set the tone of the questions, and to Heather Burns for proofreading drafts and making digital files of the Scripture-proofs used in this study guide for easy reference. These can be found at www.banneroftruth.org/store/theology/confessing-the-faith-study-guide.

Of course I must also thank Chad. I thank him for teaching me about the Westminster Standards and for discussing doctrine on demand. I am glad that he wrote *Confessing the Faith*—I have enjoyed reading it many times over. And I thank him for reading the study guide draft and for encouraging me to finish.

Finally, I am grateful for all who prayed that I would finish. Evidently God answered those prayers. Now I pray that this study guide would be useful to you.

EMILY VAN DIXHOORN

January 23, 2017

# SUGGESTIONS FOR
# GROUP LEADERS

———————

A leader helps set the tone and pace for a discussion group. Here are some ideas to consider for preparation and leading the group:

### Before the study

1. Complete the questions yourself, even if that means just jotting down a few notes.

2. To guide your pace, mark in your margin the clock-time you think the group should start each question.

3. Decide if you will need to skip some questions to keep within your time frame, and if so, which ones.

4. Note which questions can be covered quickly and which are worthy of group discussion.

5. For longer chapters, consider how many sections you will cover per meeting. A symbol is inserted at suggested break points.

6. Pray for clear understanding, for respectful interaction, and for participation from all.

## *At the study*

1. Out of respect for participants, begin and end on time. Perhaps gather with a hymn related to the topic. Don't wait for everyone to arrive before you start singing—they can join in!

2. Open your discussion with a brief prayer. Then consider using an ice-breaker question.

3. Encourage participation—don't be afraid to call on people. A friendly 'Pat, what do you think about this?' can draw a quiet person out.

4. Don't criticize poor answers—instead, encourage new ones.

5. Keep your discussion moving and on topic. Be ready to invite people to discuss a topic further outside of the group so you can move on with the study. 'This is a big issue. I'd be happy to discuss that with you later, but let's move on for now. We have a lot right here to discuss.'

6. Lead in application. Share an area where you are applying the doctrine under discussion to your life.

7. Close in prayer.

# FOUNDATIONS

# CHAPTER 1:

# OF THE HOLY SCRIPTURE

———————————

❦

## WCF 1.1

### *General revelation: conscience, creation, and providence*

1. What are the two forms of general revelation mentioned in the opening line of the confession?

2. What does general revelation declare? Support your answer with Scripture. How could this direct our evangelism and defence of the faith?

### *Special revelation: the Word of God*

3. What is the ultimate purpose of Holy Scripture and why is it necessary? How should this purpose affect how we read and study Scripture?

4. Why would the Westminster divines doubt people who claimed to have personal revelation from God?

## WCF 1.2-3

### *Holy Scripture*

    5. How is Scripture set apart from all other books? How does this inform our life and doctrine?

### *A complete canon*

    6. How might we be tempted to add or take away from the Scriptures? How is the warning in Revelation 22:18-19 relevant to this discussion?

### *An inspired book*

    7. The commentary warns that, 'Those who ignore the Holy Scripture are doomed to stumble into ever deepening darkness.' Why? What does the commentary say we should do to avoid this?

### *Apocrypha*

    8. How should Christians view the Apocrypha? If the Apocryphal books are not inspired by the Holy Spirit, should we read them at all?

## WCF 1.4-5

### *God's Word*

    9. Upon whose testimony should we trust in Scripture? How does Scripture itself support this conclusion?

### Our persuasion and assurance

10. What is some of the 'abundant evidence' which the Bible gives about itself, testifying that it is the Word of God?

11. From where does our final and full assurance in God's Word come? How can this comfort us?

12. How might your understanding of the Spirit help you respond to someone who says that we cannot know God?

### WCF 1.6

### Scripture sufficient

1. Why is it important to know that unlike any other book, Scripture is sufficient for salvation and all matters of faith?

### Good and necessary consequence

2. Give examples of what is 'expressly set down in Scripture' and what is 'deduced by good and necessary consequence'. Why do we sometimes need to make deductions? Why do we need to be careful when we do this?

### Qualifier 1: we need the Spirit

3. If we do not need new revelations of the Spirit, why do we still need the Spirit?

### Qualifier 2: worship and government

4. How should Scripture regulate our worship? How can Christian prudence inform our worship?

## WCF 1.7-8

### The clarity of Scripture

5. How might knowing that a passage of Scripture is not always clear in itself shape our study of God's Word?

6. How might knowing that not all of Scripture is 'alike clear unto all' humble us?

### Texts and translations of Scripture

7. How might knowing that God preserved his Word help you to praise him and trust his Word?

8. Even though the Hebrew and Greek texts of the Bible are the ultimate standard for any controversy in religion, why is it still a good idea to have the Scriptures translated into many different languages?

## WCF 1.9-10

### The infallible rule

9. Why is it vitally important to remember 'that the most important resource to help us understand the Bible is the Bible itself'?

10. How does knowing that God's Word is meant to be read as one book help you as you read it?

### The supreme judge

11. Why is it important to understand that Scripture is the supreme judge of spiritual things?

12. In light of your study of the Holy Scripture, how would you like to pray? For what would you like to give thanks? What do you need to confess? What do you need to request for yourself and for those under your care?

# CHAPTER 2:

# OF GOD,
# AND OF THE HOLY TRINITY

## WCF 2.1

### One God, no limit

1. How does the oneness of the Trinity fundamentally contradict relativism, or the claim that we each have our own God? (Deut. 6:4; 1 Cor. 8:4-6)

2. What are some passages of Holy Scripture that highlight God's transcendent greatness? How might reflecting on God's transcendence help us in our trials?

### The God who is spirit

3. How does God's being a spirit affect our worship of him?

### Creator and creature

4. What are some ways that the Bible clearly distinguishes between the creator and the creature? Why is this important? How is it helpful?

5. When studying who God is, why is it helpful to remember that God is both knowable and incomprehensible?

### The works of God

6. What do the works of God reveal about God's character?

## WCF 2.2

### God in himself

7. What are different ways in which God is 'unto himself all-sufficient'?

### God and us

8. What is the difference between God's 'deriving' glory from his creatures and his 'manifesting his own glory in, by, unto and upon them'?

9. What can we learn from Nebuchadnezzar about the danger of not recognizing God's sovereignty? (Dan. 4:25-35)

**WCF 2.3**

*One and three*

10. What are four ways in which the three persons of the Trinity are one?

11. According to the commentary, careless reading of the Bible can 'reduce our triune God to a grade B movie with not enough actors'. What does the commentary mean by this? What is this error traditionally called? What passages could you use to correct this defective reading of Scripture?

12. Suggest a practical way that your worship and prayers can reflect both the 'oneness' and the 'three-ness' of your triune God. Keep this in mind as you close your study in prayer.

# THE DECREES OF GOD

# CHAPTER 3:

# OF GOD'S ETERNAL DECREE

❦

**WCF 3.1-2**

*An eternal, wise and holy plan*

1. What key phrases does the confession use to describe God's decree?

*Three qualifiers*

2. What are the confession's three qualifiers to its comprehensive statement regarding God's decree?

3. How do you sometimes respond to God when his providence is not according to your plan? How would you like to respond?

4. Challenge: What consequences might follow from denying God's sovereignty over secondary causes?

### *The God who is free*

5. How might we use Holy Scripture to respond to someone who says 'God saved me because he knew that I would respond positively to the gospel'?

6. The commentary notes: 'The decree of God has been the subject of too much debate in the history of the church. The reality is that the parties in these disputes are often much closer to one another than they admit.' What are the different emphases? In what ways are the parties close to one another?

## WCF 3.3-5

### *Destinies of life and death*

7. What is God's purpose in election? What does this tell us in turn about his character?

8. According to the commentary, what three points must we remember when thinking about predestination?

### *A certain number*

9. How can we know that the number of the elect does not change?

10. Why does the Westminster Assembly give more emphasis to election than reprobation?

### A secret counsel

11. What does it mean to say that election is according to God's 'secret counsel'?

### In Christ alone

12. How does the believer's election relate to Christ as 'the chosen one of God'?

### Free grace, not foreseen faith

13. What is the difference between a divine decision resting on 'foreseen faith' and one rooted in 'free grace'?

14. How could understanding God's mercy encourage you to serve the undeserving? What opportunities do you have to show mercy—in your home, work, city or town?

15. How does understanding God's eternal decree help us to properly elevate God and humble ourselves?

🌿

## WCF 3.6

### Appointed for glory

1. As pointed out by the commentary, what 'two things' does the opening sentence of this sixth paragraph tell us?

2. The commentary notes, 'When God appoints the elect to glory, both ends and means are important'. The appointed end is glory—but what are the appointed means?

### 'By Christ' and 'in Christ'

3. Which two people feature most prominently in the story of redemption?

4. Based on your study of God's eternal decree, how would you like to pray for your spiritual growth?

5. What is the difference between being *chosen* in eternity and being *redeemed* in eternity? Why is it important to note this difference? When was redemption accomplished for God's people?

### The Holy Spirit's work

6. How does God's electing love relate to the Spirit's work in salvation?

### A blessed hope, a solemn reality

7. How is God's predestinating will in salvation both 'a blessed hope' and 'a solemn reality'?

### WCF 3.7-8

### Passed by

8. The confession points out that it was specifically *God's* plan to withhold mercy from some creatures. How does the commentary use Scripture to support this?

*This high mystery*

9. What guidance does the confession offer to help us handle the doctrine of predestination?

10. How can the doctrine of election aid a believer's growth in assurance of faith?

11. Based on your study of God's eternal decree, how would you like to pray for your spiritual growth?

CHAPTER 4:

# OF CREATION

———

✿

**WCF 4.1**

*Creation: the work of the triune God*

    1. How is each of the three persons of the Trinity involved in the work of creation? Cite particular verses.

    2. What does the fact that creation is the work of all three persons of the Trinity teach us about God?

*Creation preaches God's glory*

    3. What particular attributes of God does creation manifest?

    4. What two important points does creation 'preach' to the unbeliever? How can these points be useful when communicating the Christian faith?

### All things of nothing

5. How do we understand that God made all things of nothing? What significance might this have for Christian apologetics?

### Visible and invisible

6. What is the invisible creation? How might remembering the creation that we cannot see enrich our prayers and worship?

### In the space of six days, and all very good

7. What conclusion from Genesis 1 does the confession highlight? How might this choice of emphasis be useful to the church?

## WCF 4.2

### Creator and creature

8. How does the creation account both humble and elevate humans?

### Male and female

9. According to the commentary, what is the apex of creation? Carefully draw some implications from this point.

### Reason and immortality

10. As noted by the Westminster Confession, what are some ways that men and women are set apart from other creatures?

### The image of God

11. What makes the fall of man so horrific?

12. When discussing God's image, to what four dimensions or themes does the assembly give prominence? Why these four in particular?

13. How can the image of God serve as an equalizer in our every day attitude toward others?

### The law in our hearts

14. How was the human conscience affected by the fall? (Consider Rom. 2:14-15.)

15. At creation, what ability did humans have to keep or break the law?

### The law about the tree

16. In addition to the law written on human hearts, what law did God give at creation? Describe the condition of humans as they kept this law.

17. How does your study of creation affect your attitude toward the law today?

18. Are there any particular truths you would like to remember or apply? As you close this study, consider praising God for his work of creation.

# CHAPTER 5:

# OF PROVIDENCE

_____

❦

**WCF 5.1**

*The extent of God's providence*

1. How does the Westminster Confession describe the extent of God's providence?

2. What does the contrast between the creature and the creator in Job 38–41 teach us about God's providence?

3. What might our complaints about our problems and our lack of thanks for our blessings say about our view of God's providence?

*The goodness of providence*

4. How do we know that God's providence is 'most wise and holy'?

5. When God's providence does not seem good to us, what scriptural passages might correct our perspective?

### *The glory of God's providence*

6. What attributes of God are glorified through his providence?

## WCF 5.2-3

### *The first cause*

7. What does the confession mean by calling God, 'the first cause'?

8. What does the confession mean in stating that God uses 'second causes'?

### *Second causes: necessary, free, contingent*

9. How would you describe the three types of second causes identified by the commentary? Give a biblical example of each.

10. Can you think of an example of a second cause in your life? Of the three types above, what type of second cause is it?

### *Ordinary and less ordinary providence*

11. What passages does the commentary use to show that God ordinarily uses means to effect his sovereign will? Can you think of other passages to support this point?

12. Where does Scripture show that God is not restricted to 'ordinary providence' or normal means? What does this tell us about the character of God?

13. How could studying God's providence help us to grow in contentment?

❦

## WCF 5.4

### *The fall, and the sins of angels and men*

1. How does the goodness of God's providence relate to the fall and all other sins?

2. The commentary notes the prayer of the persecuted church in Jerusalem, remembering God's hand in Jesus' suffering (Acts 4:27-28). How might we acknowledge God's hand in our own suffering, or in the suffering of another? How could this be helpful to us? Can you think of a specific example from your experience?

### *God's permission*

3. How is God's 'permitting' sin different from simply 'not interfering' with man?

4. What Scripture does the commentary use to show God's arranging events according 'to his own holy ends'? Challenge: Can you cite additional biblical examples?

### *The holiness and innocence of God*

5. How does God underscore that he is not the author of sin?

6. What does the commentary call 'the real wonder of God's providence'? What does his providence cost him?

## WCF 5.5-7

### *Evil for good*

7. According to WCF 5.5, what are three reasons why a 'most wise, righteous, and gracious God' would leave his children in sin or suffering for a season?

### *Good for evil*

8. What does the commentary mean by saying that God, 'in a sense, even works good for evil'? What passages does the commentary use to support this point?

9. How does the commentary demonstrate the concurrence of God's sovereignty and human responsibility regarding the hardening of one's heart?

10. As the commentary notes, 'The same event, action or position can be used by one for their own good and by another for their destruction'. How might this encourage us to take responsibility for our actions?

### *The church*

11. What privileges does the church experience in regard to God's providence?

12. Consider closing your study with a prayer of thanks and praise for God's providence in general, and specifically in your life.

# SIN AND THE SAVIOUR

# CHAPTER 6

# OF THE FALL OF MAN, OF SIN, AND OF THE PUNISHMENT THEREOF

—

🌿

## WCF 6.1-2

### *The fall*

1. According to the commentary, what is 'arguably the greatest irony in history'? (Consider Rom. 11:32-33.) How could this great irony encourage you to trust God more?

2. What comfort can we find in God using human sin for his own glory? Consider if there is a particular past sin for which you need to trust God to use for your good and his glory.

### *Fallenness*

3. How does Holy Scripture describe the effects of man's sin upon himself? How is it helpful to be wise to this dynamic? How does the gospel disrupt the effects of sin?

## Death

4. How does Scripture describe the effects of sin as death? What can we do to better grasp the seriousness of our sin?

## A sad conspiracy

5. Some people seem to have their lives 'all together', seemingly untouched by the fall. Do you ever think about someone this way? How are we to understand this in light of Romans 3:10-19? What implications does this have for our evangelism and prayers of intercession?

6. Sometimes when Christians sin, we lose hope of testifying well to Christ. What does Paul's example in 1 Timothy 1:15-16 teach us about how we, as sinners, can still glorify God?

## WCF 6.3-4

### The root of all mankind

7. What does the confession mean by the term 'the root of all mankind'? How does this image help us understand sin?

8. According to the commentary, what 'very important point' does the confession make about how the effects of the fall are communicated—and how not? Why is this point so important?

## Sin

9. What is the relationship between original sin and actual sin?

10. How does Scripture describe the extremity and extent of human corruption? Do you consider the confession's summary of corruption to be fair?

11. How does understanding the severity of sin prepare us to understand the gospel?

## WCF 6.5-6

### *Remaining corruption*

12. How might we respond to one who claims to not sin? What Scriptures might we point to?

13. Instead of expecting perfection from Christians, what should we expect?

### *Original sin and actual sins*

14. According to 1 John 3:4, what is sin?

15. How does the confession echo Scripture in describing sin's effects?

16. What important difference does the commentary point out between the teaching of the Westminster divines and that of the Roman Catholic Church regarding the effects of sin? How do these respective teachings compare with Scripture?

17. On what hopeful note does the commentary end this discussion of sin? Consider closing your study praying that in the face of sin, you would both have hope in Christ and share that hope with others.

# CHAPTER 7:

# OF GOD'S COVENANT WITH MAN

⸻

🌿

**WCF 7.1-2**

*A distance so great*

1. How does Scripture describe the distance between God and man?

2. What images does Scripture use to express that God does not need us?

3. How do these twin truths—first, that there is a great distance between the natures of God and man, and second, that God does not need man—set the stage for discussing God's covenant with man?

*A covenant*

4. In most basic terms, what is a covenant?

5. What elements of a covenant do we see in the garden of Eden?

## *A covenant of works*

6. The commentary points out that the first covenant is often termed a 'covenant of works'. How does Scripture emphasize works when describing God's covenant with Adam?

## WCF 7.3-4

### *The covenant of grace*

7. Why is the new covenant called a 'covenant of grace'?

8. As noted in the commentary, how do both the covenant of works and the covenant of grace express God's gracious character?

9. What is the substance or centre of the covenant of grace?

10. What does God require of man in the covenant of grace? (See Rom. 10:9; Gal. 3:11; Mark 16:16.)

11. What does the commentary advise us to remember when our faith waivers?

## *A testament?*

12. The commentary notes that the *Septuagint* (Greek translation of the Old Testament) refers to the covenant by the term 'testament'. How does the idea of 'testament'

underscore the gospel message? (Consider Heb. 7:22; 9:15-17; Luke 22:20; 1 Cor. 11:25.)

❦

## WCF 7.5-6

### *The Old Testament*

1. How was the covenant of grace administered differently in the time of the law and the time of the gospel? (See 2 Cor. 3:7-9.)

2. As explained in the commentary, what is 'the redeeming feature of this time of the law'?

3. How does circumcision point to Christ? (See Col. 2:11-12 and Rom. 4:11.)

4. How did the Passover point to Christ? (Consider 1 Cor. 5:7.)

5. How does Scripture show that the substance of faith is the same in the Old and New Testaments? (See John 8:56; Heb. 11:13; Gal. 3:7-9, 14.) Why does this matter?

### *The New Testament*

6. Why is the focus of proper preaching and administration of the sacraments always only Christ? Use Scripture to support your answer.

7. What explanation does the commentary give for why the new dispensation of the covenant is greater than the old?

(Consider Heb. 12:22-24; Jer. 31:33-34; Matt. 18:19; Eph. 2:15-19.)

8. The confession states that there are not 'two covenants of grace differing in substance' but rather there is 'one and the same' under various dispensations. Can this be demonstrated from Scripture? If so, how?

9. How does recognizing the unity of the old and new covenants, in addition to the superiority of the new, give you reason to thank and praise God? Consider closing your study expressing this in prayer.

# CHAPTER 8:

# OF CHRIST THE MEDIATOR

━━━━━━━━━━━━━

❧

**WCF 8:1**

## *The mediator*

1. How does Scripture confirm the confession's statement that God was pleased to choose Christ as the mediator? What do you find significant about this choice?

## *Prophet, Priest and King*

2. What are some passages that reveal Christ in his three offices as mediator—as prophet, priest and king? Are there ways in which Christ fulfils these functions that benefit you from day to day?

3. The commentary notes, 'This threefold office of Christ as prophet, priest and king together with his headship over the church has vast implications for the way we consider his church. Plainly, it ought to shape how we think and speak of it, how we order it, how we serve in it, and how we

worship in it…' How does the fact that Christ is prophet, priest, king, and head over the church shape your service in the church? (Consider Eph. 5:23.)

4. The commentary notes, 'With the Son of God as a mediator between God and man, what Christian has a right to be afraid of death and judgment?' What security do you receive from Christ's ministry of mediation? How might you use this doctrine to help someone who is afraid of death?

### The gift

5. How does Scripture describe the church as a gift to Christ? Why does the commentary call this gift 'a wonder'?

6. How might recognizing that God's people are a gift to Christ give us a reason to repent thoroughly of our sins?

7. Section 8.1 closes with a list of benefits Christ achieves for his people over time. How does God's mighty power to transform people encourage you today? (Consider 1 Tim. 2:6; 1 Cor. 1:30; Isa. 55:4-5.)

## WCF 8.2

### God and man

8. What are some passages that reveal Christ's divinity? His humanity?

9. The commentary reminds us that the incarnation 'is not a case of man becoming God (which will never happen). This is God becoming man.' Why is this an important distinction?

10. The commentary notes that we must understand the words that we use. What adjectives does the confession use to describe the two natures of Christ and what do they mean?

11. The confession states that the two distinct natures of Christ were inseparably joined together in one person 'without conversion, composition, or confusion'. What does each of these terms mean?

    • Without conversion

    • Without composition

    • Without confusion

12. How might a better understanding of Christ's divinity and humanity help a believer endure physical suffering? Resist temptation? Are there ways you have been helped by reflection on Christ's person?

## WCF 8.3

### *The Holy Spirit*

1. How is Christ unique in his experience of the Holy Spirit? (See John 3:34.)

2. What scriptural evidence do we have that Jesus was full of the Spirit? Why did Christ need to be full of the Spirit?

3. Sometimes people think since we can't be perfect, there is no point in trying at all. How might understanding Christ's relation to the Spirit help us not to give up?

### Christ as 'surety'

4. How does the author of Hebrews describe Christ as 'surety' or 'guarantor'? (See Heb. 12:24; Heb. 7:22; Heb. 5:4-5.) What hope can you find offered by this description?

5. The commentator notes, 'It would be a mistake to think of the mediator only in his weakness, and not in his strength.'

(a) How do we need Christ as mediator in his weakness?

(b) How do we need Christ as mediator in his strength? (See Matt. 28:18; John 5:22, 27; Acts 2:36.)

(c) Do you tend to think of him more in one way than another? How would you like to think about him more?

## WCF 8.4

### A willing mediator

6. Why did Jesus, as mediator, need to be born 'under the law'? (See Gal. 4:4.)

7. How can the knowledge that Christ fulfilled the law perfectly in our place help us face our failures? How can it encourage our obedience?

*Torments of the soul, suffering of the body / A risen Saviour*

8. Describe the range of experience that Christ had and still has as mediator, as summarized in WCF 8.4. Support with Scripture as you are able.

*An ascended Saviour*

9. The commentary warns us 'not to busy ourselves judging one another. The Lord will do this for us.' How can knowing Christ as your mediator guard you against a judgmental spirit? (Consider Acts 10:42 and Rom. 14:9-10.)

10. What is one truth you would like to remember regarding Christ as mediator? Why is it important to you? As you close your study, consider praying with thanks, asking God to help you apply this truth to your life.

❦

## WCF 8.5

*Fully satisfied justice*

1. How is your conscience affected by knowing that Christ perfectly satisfied God's justice? (See Heb. 9:14.)

2. What two benefits did Christ purchase for his people through his sacrifice? What 'benefit' does Christ receive from the Father through his sacrifice for us? Does this amaze you—if so, why?

3. How does knowing that when God reconciles himself to man, he does so completely, comfort you? How does it challenge you as a peacemaker among people?

4. How can you honour the labour of Christ that earned you a clean conscience?

## WCF 8.6

### *Redemption applied or 'communicated'*

5. What are some similarities and differences between faith before the incarnation and after? How does Scripture point to these?

6. In the midst of the various changes we experience, how can knowing that Jesus Christ does not change give us peace? Can you think of a way this truth gives you peace in your present circumstances?

## WCF 8.7

### *One person, two natures / It is a person who saves us*

7. How does Scripture demonstrate that Christ, as mediator, worked according to both his human and divine nature? (Consider Heb. 9:14; 1 Pet. 3:1, as well as additional passages.)

### *The communication of attributes*

8. What is meant by the 'communication of attributes'? What is not meant?

### *Biblical language*

9. How does Scripture sometimes ascribe an attribute of one nature to the other nature? What is the confession's purpose in pointing this out?

10. What is hard to understand about the second person of the Trinity? What is more clear and easier to understand? Why is this distinction helpful to recognize?

11. How should the fact that our Saviour is in some ways beyond our understanding shape the way we respond to his providence and his commands?

## WCF 8.8

### *A certain and effective application*

12. What does the confession mean by saying that Christ 'certainly and effectively' applies redemption to his people? (Consider John 6:37-39 and John 10:15-16 for scriptural support.) What comfort can we receive from this? How can this truth help us to live honestly before God?

### *Christ's interceding and revealing*

13. How does Christ's intercession add security to our salvation? (Consider 1 John 2:1-2 and Rom. 8:34.)

14. How does Christ's intercession set an example for your prayers?

### The effectual work of Christ's Spirit

15. The commentary calls the Spirit 'indispensable' to all we are and hope to be. What does the Spirit do to make Christ's work on the cross effective? (Consider 2 Cor. 4:13; Rom. 8:9-14; Rom 15:18-19; John 17:17.)

16. If we don't feel full of the Spirit, why, according to the commentary, might that be? How can we tell if we actually are or are not full of the Spirit?

### Overcoming all

17. How does Scripture describe God's overcoming all of his and our enemies? (Consider Psa. 110:1; 1 Cor. 15:25-26; Mal. 4:2-3; Col. 2:15.)

18. Why can this be useful to remember, especially given conflicts in the world today?

19. Based on Christ's work as a mediator, what are some reasons why we should leave judgment to God?

20. How will you thank God for the work of Christ as mediator?

# SALVATION

# CHAPTER 9:

# OF FREE WILL

━━━━━━

❦

**WCF 9.1**

*A natural liberty, unforced*

1. How does Scripture support the idea that man has 'natural
   liberty'?

*A natural liberty, without natural determination*

2. The commentary cautions us: 'we must not forget that the
   will still really does have the power of self-decision'. When
   might you forget the power of self-decision, for yourself
   or others? What is the danger of forgetting this?

*The will in any state*

3. What does James 1:14 teach us about our will? How might
   this truth facilitate true repentance?

## *A difficult doctrine*

4. Understanding the topic free will in light of God's sovereignty has challenged people of all backgrounds and through all ages. How did Burgess, one of the Westminster divines, describe the difficulty of this topic, and how would you? How does the commentary direct us to pray as we approach this challenging topic?

5. How does the presence of 'free will'—though in some sense only—expand the way we should pray for ourselves and others?

## WCF 9.2-3

### *Innocence*

6. How does the confession organize its discussion of human will in 9.2–9.5? Why is this important?

7. What were Adam and Eve free and able to do in their state of innocence?

### *The fall*

8. How does Genesis demonstrate that, after the fall, Adam and Eve 'wholly lost all ability of will to [do] any spiritual good accompanying salvation'?

### *Fallen man*

9. How does reflection on the human will after the fall help you to understand the need for God's grace more clearly?

**WCF 9.4-5**

*Free to will what is good*

10. How does God's saving work change our will?

*Free to will what is evil*

11. Are you surprised when you see a believer sin? Should we be? Why or why not?

*Free to do good alone!*

12. What does Scripture have to say about the change to the believer's will upon Christ's return?

13. In terms of the human will, how is this final stage of history the best of all? Contrast this last stage to all prior stages.

14. In closing, consider praying for the ongoing sanctification of the will, thanking God for the benefits that we gain at Christ's return, and praying that the Lord would come quickly.

# CHAPTER 10:

# OF EFFECTUAL CALLING

**WCF 10.1**

*Predestination and the divine call*

1. What does it mean to say that God's call is always effective? How does Scripture communicate this point?

*By Word and Spirit*

2. How do Word and Spirit complement one another in God's effectual call? How are they both necessary? Use Scripture to support your answer.

3. How do we sometimes neglect either Word or Spirit? How can we be careful to give each its due place?

*Out of sin and death, into grace and salvation*

4. What is the role of other believers in God's effectual call?

5. What impact does God's call have on us? Where would we be without God's call? What place does God's call have in your description of the gospel?

### The mind, the heart, the will

6. How does God make his call effective? (See Acts 26:18; and 1 Cor. 2:10-12.) How then should we pray?

7. The commentary notes, 'For many Christians, the scriptural teaching on God's effectual call is full of comfort.' How does the doctrine of effectual calling provide comfort for believers and reassurance for preachers?

## WCF 10.2

### God's grace and our helplessness

8. As noted by the commentary, what is the shift of focus from the first paragraph to the second? How does the second build on the first?

9. What does the confession mean by describing God's effectual call as 'free', 'special', and of 'grace alone'? How might we reflect these qualities in our discipleship and evangelism?

10. The commentary notes, 'One way in which God underlines his grace is to set it repeatedly beside our helplessness.' In discussing salvation, how does Scripture make this contrast? (You might consider Eph. 2:4-9; 2 Tim. 1:9; Titus 3:4-5; Rom. 9:11.) Can you identify a situation in your life where your helplessness has magnified God's grace?

11. The commentary notes an erroneous view of God's call, namely that God saves a person because he 'peered into the future and noticed that certain people would have religious insight where others would not'. How might you use Scripture to correct this error? Point out both what is wrong with this view and offer a positive correction.

### Made alive

12. How does Scripture shed light on the confession's claim that a person cannot answer God's call until being 'quickened' or 'made alive' and 'renewed'? (See 1 Cor. 2:14; Rom. 8:9; Eph. 2:5.)

### Answering the call

13. If we do not answer God's call, that call is of no use to us. We might worry that we will miss God's call. How does Scripture assure us that all of God's children will answer God's call?

❧

## WCF 10.3

### Elect infants

1. According to the commentary, what is 'the whole point of this chapter on effectual calling'? What is the focus of this particular section? How does remembering the point of the chapter help us understand this section?

2. How might we sometimes emphasize age and ability over the power of God's call? By way of contrast, how does Scripture emphasize God's power over human ability?

3. The commentary states that 'the non-negotiable for salvation is not faith'. What is the non-negotiable? What is the point of this emphasis?

4. What does the commentary identify as two points that the WCF does not teach regarding infants and the mentally inhibited child? In simple terms, what are the similarities and differences between the salvation of an elect infant and that of an elect adult? (Consider Acts 4:12 among other verses.)

5. Even if we cannot know if an infant is elect or not, where can we turn for hope, confidence, and comfort?

## WCF 10.4

### The non-elect

6. In comparison to the previous paragraphs, what is the 'new angle' this paragraph takes on effectual calling?

7. What does the confession mean by saying that some 'may have common operations of the Spirit, yet they never truly come to Christ'? How does Jesus demonstrate his awareness of this sad condition? How should we?

8. How does the world suggest that God accepts good people? What does Scripture teach regarding God's view of them?

9. What was the Apostle Paul's attitude toward any teaching contrary to salvation through Christ alone? How should we respond to such error?

10. What makes the teaching of Chapter 10 of the confession difficult? What makes it compelling? As you close your study, consider giving thanks to God for areas of increased clarity and pray for faithfulness to the challenging truths herein.

# CHAPTER 11:

# OF JUSTIFICATION

────────────

❧

**WCF 11.1**

*A free justification*

1. How does the Westminster Assembly connect Effectual Calling in Chapter 10 and Justification in Chapter 11? Why is this connection important?

*Justification: what it is not and what it is*

2. Some have said that to be justified is to be 'just as if we never sinned'. According to the commentary, how can this statement be improved? (See Rom. 3:22-28.)

*The grounds of justification: not because of us, but because of Christ*

3. What Old and New Testament passages point out that our justification is because of Christ, not us?

### *Saving righteousness: not our faith or obedience, but Christ's*

4. According to the commentary, what have Arminians traditionally affirmed about justification, and how does the confession contrast this view? How might these different views of justification, if taken to their logical conclusion, work themselves out in different attitudes toward God?

### *Justified by faith*

5. How does Scripture support the confession's statement that believers are justified by faith as a gift from God? How should this humble us?

## WCF 11.2-3

### *Faith alone*

6. Some people say that we are justified by faith, but that our works also contribute to our justification. Even if we don't believe in such works righteousness, can you detect a way that functionally, you look to your works for your acceptance before God? What problems arise from this pattern? In contrast, how does Scripture present faith as the only instrument of justification? And what are the benefits of justification for believers?

### *Faith never alone*

7. The commentary points out an irony: believers are justified by faith alone, but 'that faith is never alone in the person justified'. Explain the meaning of this phrase, using Scripture to support your answer.

### Christ's obedience and death

8. What does it mean to say that Christ made a 'proper, real, and full satisfaction' to his Father's justice in behalf of his people? How does Scripture support these terms? Why is understanding this important to a believer?

9. Why does God's grace sometimes seem too good to be true? (Consider Rom. 3:24 and Eph. 1:7 in your answer.) What should be our response to this great gift?

## WCF 11.4-6

### Justification in eternity?

10. How does Scripture point to an eschatological aspect to justification? How does this eternal dimension to justification bring glory to God? What comfort do you receive from this? (Consider Gal. 3.8; 1 Pet. 1:2, 19-20; Rom. 8:30.)

### Justification in history

11. The commentary points out that in emphasizing either God's eternal decree or Christ's death and resurrection, some have unfortunately lost sight of the fact that justification actually occurs at a point in time in the life of the person justified. What harm can come from missing this fact? How does Scripture emphasize a turning point in a believer's life?

*Saved sinners*

12. Where does Scripture tell us that justified people still sin? What problems might we face if we thought that once justified, believers didn't sin anymore?

13. How does Scripture demonstrate that believers cannot fall out of a state of justification? How might knowing that believers remain in a state of justification help you to confess your sins more fully and freely? How does a believer's security in Christ glorify God? How can it help you enjoy God more?

*A Father's discipline*

14. Can you describe a time when you experienced God's fatherly displeasure in a way that eventually led you to renew your faith and repentance?

*The old and new Testaments*

15. In reference to WCF 11.6, the commentary states, 'God's salvation is one and the same through all time unto eternity.' How does Hebrews 13:8 reinforce this point? Identify the essential elements of justification present in both the old and new Testaments.

16. Given the doctrine of justification, how would you like to praise God? How would you like to pray for yourself?

# CHAPTER 12:

# OF ADOPTION

## *Blessings as a package*

1. How does Scripture reveal that adoption has long been God's purpose?

2. What does the commentary mean by saying that 'the saving blessings and graces that come from Jesus Christ always come as a package'? Why is it helpful to remember this when studying adoption?

## *The uniqueness of adoption*

3. What makes the blessing of adoption distinct from justification and sanctification? What makes it similar?

4. How does Scripture highlight the privilege of adoption? (See Rom. 8:17 and John 1:12.)

### Called by the Father's name

5. How should the fact that a Christian bears the family name affect our public behaviour? Our private thoughts?

6. How does Scripture describe the Holy Spirit's role in adoption?

7. How does knowing God as Father reinforce his other names?

### Chastisement

8. What does Scripture teach us about God's fatherly discipline?

9. Consider the benefits of adoption listed in WCF 12. If you had to choose, on which benefit would you want to meditate further for your own encouragement?

### Father and children

10. How should remembering that we are part of God's family affect our fellowship with other believers? (Consider Heb. 1:14.)

11. In the light of your study on adoption, how would you like to pray for yourself? How would you like to pray for others?

CHAPTER 13:

# OF SANCTIFICATION

**WCF 13.1**

*Regeneration and sanctification*

1. What is the first necessary step to sanctification? How does
   Scripture describe this step?

2. Is sanctification a necessary grace or an optional bonus
   in the Christian life? What do your actions say about the
   importance of sanctification in the believer? What does
   Scripture say?

3. The commentary stresses, 'It is important to remember that
   sanctification is God's work because Christians sometimes
   summarize salvation as if one part of its progress is to be
   credited to God and one part to us.' How does Scripture
   emphasize that sanctification is God's work, accomplished
   only through union with Christ?

## Word and Spirit

4. How does Scripture describe the role of Word and Spirit in sanctification?

## Destroying the dominion of sin

5. Given that both Word and Spirit are essential to sanctification, what would you expect to see in a life that is being sanctified?

6. What biblical language describes sanctification as a mortification of sin? How can our attitude towards sin reflect this? Is there a specific sin you need to crucify?

## Being strengthened in saving graces

7. If crucifying sin is one part of sanctification, what is the other? How is it helpful to remember both aspects?

## WCF 13.2-3

## Sanctification throughout

8. What is the purpose of this section in comparison to the previous one?

9. What does the confession mean by the statement 'Sanctification is for the whole man'? When it comes to sanctification, is there an area of your life that you consider 'off limits'? How would you apply a passage such as 1 Thessalonians 5:23 to this area?

### Remaining corruption

10. How does Scripture refute perfectionism—the idea that people can completely get rid of sin in this life?

### A necessary war

11. What is the war that engages every Christian? What does Scripture tell us about this war? How can remembering this war help us live at peace with one another?

### Growing in grace

12. The commentary notes that it might not feel as if Christians are growing spiritually even when we are. If feelings can't accurately indicate spiritual growth, what can? How does Scripture support this experience of Christian growth? Can you identify a period when you grew spiritually but didn't feel as if you were at the time?

13. Amidst the ongoing battle of sanctification, our desire to grow in grace can wax and wane. How should we respond to this? What can we do to avoid going through the motions of religion and, instead, engage our hearts in our spiritual disciplines? (Consider 2 Pet. 3:18.)

14. In closing this study, consider Paul's exhortation in 2 Corinthians 7:1. How would you like to pray for your sanctification? How would you like to pray for the sanctification of others under your care?

# CHAPTER 14:

# OF SAVING FAITH

⟨❧⟩

**WCF 14.1**

*Faith*

1. What are two biblical meanings of the word 'faith'? How does Scripture support these meanings?

*The work of the Spirit*

2. Where does saving faith come from? What implication does this have for our evangelism?

*The ordinary means*

3. When we recognize that our faith is weak, what do the Apostles Peter and Paul advise us to do? What implication might this have for the way we schedule ministries in the church that could keep someone from attending public worship?

## *The sacraments and prayer*

4. How has your faith been strengthened by witnessing or participating in baptism and the Lord's supper?

## WCF 14.2-3

## *Faith in the Word of God*

5. In comparison with the first paragraph, what is the aim of this second paragraph of Chapter 14?

6. What does faith do? Support your answer with examples from Scripture.

## *Obeying, fearing and embracing the Word*

7. The commentary states that 'if passages have different emphases, they may require different responses'. What does the commentator mean by this statement? Can you think of any examples of your own that would illustrate the truth of it?

8. What does the commentator mean by riding a hobby-horse? How can we avoid this problem in our own Bible reading and teaching?

## *Faith in Christ*

9. What is the focus of faith?

10. What is the difference between looking to the benefits that come from Christ and looking to Christ himself?

### *Faith that grows*

11. How does Scripture portray varying degrees of faith?

12. Where should our confidence be placed—in the strength of our faith or elsewhere?

13. In closing your study, consider praying for specific growth of your own faith and of the faith of those under your care.

# CHAPTER 15:

# OF REPENTANCE UNTO LIFE

🌿

## WCF 15.1-2

### *Repentance that leads to life*

1. What are two ways in which repentance is an evangelical or 'gospel' grace?

2. Where in Scripture do we see people preaching repentance unto life? Have you heard the message of repentance preached recently? If so, how was it presented?

### *Turning from sin and turning to God*

3. How does Scripture present the urgency for repentance?

4. What does the commentary mean by calling sin a '*personal* affair'. How could we add a personal dimension to our repentance?

5. How does the commentary describe the difference between remorse and repentance? What Scripture supports this point?

## WCF 15.3-4

### *Repentance as 'self-satisfaction' or the 'cause' of pardon?*

6. Can you detect a way that you slip into a mind-set of penance—of 'paying for' your own sins through pious deeds rather than receiving God's pardon as a gift? How can we tell which mind-set we have?

### *God's free grace in Christ*

7. How does Scripture emphasize God's free grace as the ground of our pardon? What impact does this have on your attitude and character?

### *The necessity of repentance*

8. Can there be salvation if someone believes in the triune God and the facts of the gospel, yet does not engage in true repentance? Use Scripture to explain why or why not.

### *Comfort for sinners*

9. Sometimes we try to comfort ourselves by making our sin look smaller than it is. What does Scripture say about the impact of sin? In the face of our sin, what comfort does Scripture offer us? What phrases particularly comfort you?

## WCF 15.5-6

### *General and particular repentance*

10. Use Scripture to describe the difference between general and particular repentance. What two aspects of particular repentance does the commentary point out?

11. When repenting, when might it be unhelpful to recall all the details of a particular sin? When might it be helpful to include the details?

### *Public and private repentance*

12. When should repentance be public and when should it be private? What are the benefits of each?

13. When someone repents of a sin against us, what is our duty before God? How do we express this? What would it look like for you to improve in this? (Consider 2 Cor. 2:7-8.)

14. What would you like to remember from your study on repentance? In light of this, how would you like a friend to pray for you?

CHAPTER 16:

# OF GOOD WORKS

---

ⓦ

## WCF 16.1-2

### *Good works that God commands*

1. How is Chapter 16 different from all previous chapters in the confession? How does Chapter 16 relate to the previous ones?

2. What good works does God command in Micah 6:8? How do these good works relate to your every day life?

### *Good works devised by men*

3. In regard to worship, how do mere good intentions fall short of pleasing God?

4. How do we sometimes give good intentions too much weight when evaluating a work? Can you think of a specific time you did this? What can be the consequences?

## *The value of good works*

5. According to the commentary, what is one way of 'keeping from the snare of a man-made piety'? (See James 2:18-22.)

6. How can we either overvalue or undervalue good works? What are seven purposes of good works, as outlined in paragraph 2? On which of these seven purposes do you want to reflect further?

## WCF 16.3-4

### *Depending on the Spirit*

7. How do paragraphs 3 and 4 build on paragraphs 1 and 2?

8. What does Scripture say about our dependence upon the Spirit for our good works?

9. How do we sometimes underestimate the importance of the work of the Spirit in our good works? How can we correct this error?

### *Stirring up God's grace*

10. The confession states that believers 'ought to be diligent in stirring up the grace of God that is in them'. How does Scripture support this? What are some practical ways we can stir up the grace of God?

11. How does 2 Peter 1:3-11 relate the Spirit's working and our working?

### The limits of good works

12. What does Nehemiah, by his good example, remind us about the limits of our good works? (See Neh. 13:22.)

13. What is 'supererogation'? Is it possible? Why or why not?

14. How could you express the gospel in terms of good works?

❦

## WCF 16.5

### Our best works and God's best: why we cannot merit eternal life

1. What are two ways Paul rules out the possibility that any part of salvation is by works?

2. When evaluating our good works, what is 'an all-important reference point'? How does this reference point guide us?

3. WCF 16.5 states 'when we have done all we can, we have done but our duty, and are unprofitable servants'. How can this perspective help us resist bitterness? Is this your perspective? Where would you like to adopt it more?

### A debt to the Spirit

4. When we recognize the fruit of the Spirit in our lives (Gal. 5:22-23), how can we give him the credit? Have you seen someone do this well?

**WCF 16.6-7**

### *The good works of believers: accepted in Christ*

5. What question do these sections try to answer? How would you answer this question, based on Scripture?

6. How does the Old Testament sacrificial system reveal that, after the fall, works were never an effective way to God?

7. How is God gracious when judging believers? Choose two or more passages to support your point, noting any that particularly encourage you. How should we respond to this gracious judge?

### *The good works of unbelievers: useful, but unacceptable, and necessary*

8. How does God acknowledge the good work of unbelievers? How can this inform the way in which we speak about others and their actions?

9. Are you willing to rejoice over good works done with less than good motives? Why or why not? Consider the example of the Apostle Paul.

10. What do Cain and Abel teach us about God's judgment of the heart? (Compare Gen. 4:5 with Heb. 11:4, 6.) How might recognizing God's perfect judgment of the heart enable you to judge more graciously?

11. According to the commentary, what are three ways that unregenerate people's works fall short?

12. How should a Christian's motive for good works be different from a non-Christian's? How is a Christian's reward different? (See Matt. 6:2, 5, 16.) How does this reward affect your work?

13. How should believers respond to God's gracious judgment? Given God's judgment, what is your prayer for unbelieving neighbours, family and friends? Consider praying for others in light of one or more of the following passages: Job 21:14-15; Matt. 25:41-45; Matt. 23:23.

CHAPTER 17:

# OF THE PERSEVERANCE
# OF THE SAINTS

———————

♨

**WCF 17.1**

*What God has done*

1. How would you express WCF 17.1 in simple terms, as if to a young child?

2. What logic does Paul use to assure the Philippians that they will persevere? Why is this a solid basis for assurance? (See Phil. 1:6.) How could you encourage with this truth?

*What God will do*

3. What duty does the believer have in regard to his perseverance? (Consider 2 Pet. 1:5-10, esp. verses 5, 10.)

4. Describe the difference between what the commentator calls 'a bare doctrine of preservation' and 'a biblical doctrine of perseverance'.

5. Should someone who confesses Christ, but over time does not show any growth in sanctification, be assured that he or she will persevere until the end? Why or why not?

6. What does God promise in 1 Peter 1:5? The commentator points out that there is only one way to live this life and life eternal: by 'God's power'. How is living by God's power different than living by any other power? What deliberate choices can you make to live by God's power?

## WCF 17.2-3

### *How Christians persevere*

7. According to paragraph 2, what is one thing on which the perseverance of saints does *not* depend, and four things on which it does? How can this encourage you?

8. How does the doctrine of perseverance give glory to God's electing love?

9. What is the unique role of each person of the Trinity in the Christian's perseverance? Support your answer with Scripture. Of what significance is it to you that all three persons of the Trinity are at work in the Christian's perseverance?

10. How does Scripture support a certain and infallible knowledge that the Lord's people will not fall away? How then are we to understand someone who confesses faith, but at a later point denies Christ our Saviour and Lord?

*Temptation, hard hearts, and scandals*

11. Does the presence of great and grievous sins indicate that a person will not persevere in the faith? How does Scripture answer this?

12. How does WCF 17.3 describe the effect of sin on a believer's relationship with the Father and with the Holy Spirit? How does Scripture?

13. How do we Christians sometimes neglect the means of our perseverance? Can you recognize any graces or comforts you have missed recently as a result of neglecting the means to your perseverance, in either large or small ways?

14. How might you warn someone against neglecting the means to his perseverance? What are the negative consequences believers may experience when neglecting the means to perseverance, as expressed in WCF 17.3 and Scripture?

15. Of the warnings above, is there a particular one you need to heed? With this in mind, consider thanking God for his promises and praying that you might be diligent in your faith.

CHAPTER 18:

# OF THE ASSURANCE OF GRACE AND SALVATION

◌

**WCF 18.1-2**

*Hypocrisy*

1. How does the commentary relate Chapter 18 on assurance to Chapter 17 on perseverance?

2. How does Scripture warn us against presumption and self-deception? Which warnings speak most powerfully to you?

*The certainty of God's grace*

3. How does WCF 18.1 contrast the presumptuous against those with an assurance of faith?

4. Does God want his children to have assurance of faith? (See 1 John 5:13.) What benefit is there to having assurance of faith? Some claim that only a few people are able to have this assurance, and that only in old age. How would you respond to this claim?

## *What kind of assurance?*

5. What does Scripture teach us about the relationship between personal sanctification and assurance of salvation? How can our assurance of salvation remain infallible even when we fail? (For help, see 2 Pet. 1:4-5, 10-11; 1 John 2:3; 1 John 3:14; 2 Cor. 1:12; Heb. 6:12-18.)

6. How does the Spirit uniquely contribute to our assurance? (See Rom. 5:15-16; Eph. 1:13-14; 4:20; 2 Cor. 1:21-22.)

## WCF 18.3

## *An unsure faith*

7. How does Scripture acknowledge that there are true believers who don't have full assurance? How does the confession discuss this in paragraph 3? How is this language helpful? What danger could there be in misunderstanding this point?

## *Finding light in darkness*

8. Although steady assurance of faith is not given to all Christians, what does 2 Peter 1:10 command all Christians to do? What are practical ways you can obey this command? How do you help those under your care to obey this as well? Where do you see room to improve? (See 2 Pet. 1:5-9.)

9. What rewards are there to diligence in confirming our election? (See Rom. 5:1-2, 5; 14:17; 15:13; Eph. 1:3-4; Psa. 4:6-7; 119:32.) Which rewards particularly encourage you?

### Carefree but not careless

10. The commentary says that 'Some people worry that if we are sure about our salvation that we will live carelessly.' How do Scripture and the confession correct this misunderstanding?

## WCF 18.4

### Our sin and God's sovereignty

11. What are four reasons Christians lack assurance of salvation, as presented in paragraph 4?

12. If someone lacks spiritual assurance, is it necessarily that person's fault? If not, why not? Give reasons from Scripture.

### Light in the darkness

13. What 'glimmers of godliness', as the commentary points out, can you detect amidst accounts of spiritual depression expressed in Scripture?

14. Read 1 John 3:9. How does knowing that a believer can always find a 'seed of God' (WCF 18.4) planted within give hope amidst spiritual depression, sin, and temptation? Can you describe a challenging time for you when you still experienced this hope?

15. What are some of the ways God revives his children's assurance, supporting them from utter despair? (See either Micah 7:7-9; Jer. 32:40; Isa. 54:7-10, or Psa. 88 for help.)

16. How would you describe your own assurance? Do you have a sure hope that you belong to God, now, and forever? If so, consider thanking God in prayer. If not, consider what you might do to grow in assurance and pray for God's help and comfort. Consider asking a pastor or elder to speak with you and pray for you.

# LAW AND LIBERTY

---

Chapter 19: Of the Law of God
(Two Studies)

Chapter 20: Of Christian Liberty, and
Liberty of Conscience
(Two Studies)

# CHAPTER 19:

# OF THE LAW OF GOD

WCF 19.1-2

### God's gift to Adam

1. In what form was the law given prior to the fall?

### Law and covenant

2. According to WCF 19.1, what are four characteristics of the obedience that God requires of us? How does Scripture express these requirements?

3. What do law and covenant have in common? What are some differences?

4. According to the commentary, how are we to understand the Apostle Paul's use of the term 'law' in Romans 10:5? With this in mind, where should we put our hope?

## *The perfect rule, pre- and post-fall*

5. How does Scripture demonstrate that after the fall the law continues to be a perfect rule of righteousness (WCF 19.2)? What illustration does George Hendry use to portray the law's continuous perfection? Can you think of any other illustrations?

6. In contrast to WCF 19.2, what voices today tell us that God's law is less than perfect? What standards do we sometimes substitute for God's law? Is there an area where you need correction and where you need to give the law its due place?

7. The commentary notes the 'interconnected unity' of God's law (Exod. 34:1; Deut. 10:4), whether inscribed on men's hearts, engraved on two tablets of stone or summarized in Jesus' two commandments. How does Scripture portray the unified character of the law? How would you in your own words? How does this unified character encourage your obedience?

## WCF 19.3-4

### The ceremonial law

8. What are three kinds of Old Testament law?

9. What analogy does the confession use to describe the reason for the ceremonial law for Israel? How does this reflect the Scripture's own teaching?

### Laws of worship and morality

10. What are the two kinds of symbols in Old Testament ceremonial law? Give examples of each kind of symbol and what they symbolized.

### The end of the ceremonial law

11. What does Scripture teach about the end of the ceremonial law? Although it has ended, what limited use does it still have for the Christian church?

### Judicial laws

12. Are Old Testament judicial laws in force today? Are they in anyway relevant today? (See 1 Pet. 2:13-14.)

13. How does the New Testament demonstrate an ongoing respect for the spirit (or underlying principles) of Old Testament judicial laws? How do these laws relate to the gospel?

## WCF 19.5

### The moral law

1. What are some New Testament passages that indicate the binding nature of the moral law? What does God's character as creator teach us about the moral law?

2. Reflecting on the unity of God's law expressed in James 2:10-11, the commentary asks: 'Why are that idea and that passage so important to this discussion about our continued obligation to the moral law?' How would you answer this in your own words?

3. As noted by the commentary, what are three misunderstandings that lead some people to say that the moral law is dissolved or reconstituted in the new covenant era? How would you use Scripture to show that Christ, in the gospel, actually strengthens our obligation to the moral law?

## WCF 19.6

### Not under the law

4. What are three uses of the moral law, as summarized by the commentary? What are we told are not legitimate uses of the moral law?

5. Are there ways that you use the law to condemn yourself? To justify yourself? What are some signs that you may be using the law in these ways?

### The first use of the law: a rule of life

6. What does Scripture teach about the relationship between the law and God's guidance? What verses particularly help you to understand this? (For help, see Rom. 7:12, 22, 25; Psa. 119:4-6; 1 Cor. 7:19; Gal. 5:14, 16, 18-23.)

### *The second use of the law: a sign-post to Christ*

7. Can you describe a recent time when the law helped you to recognize your sin? If you cannot remember a time, read the Ten Commandments or 1 Thessalonians 5:12-22 prayerfully, asking the Lord to reveal one of your particular sins.

8. When the law shows us our sin, what does Scripture say should be our response? How do we sometimes respond instead?

9. How does the law not only convict us of our sin, but also point us to Christ? (See Gal. 3:24; Rom. 7:24-25; 8:3-4.)

### *The third use of the law: a restraint for sin*

10. How do the threats and promises in the law still serve God's children who have already been saved from condemnation (WCF 19.6-7) and are already justified by faith? How does Scripture support the confession's teaching?

### *The rewards of the law*

11. How do the law's promises under the covenant of grace differ from those under the covenant of works?

### *Promises and threats as motivations for Christians*

12. How might you respond to the criticism that a person motivated by the law is relatively superficial and immature—not living by God's grace and power? (For help, see Rom. 6:12, 14; 1 Pet. 3:8-12 with Psa. 34:12-16, and Heb. 12:28-29.)

13. What implications might this chapter have on rules in the home, school, or workplace? Consider what kinds of motivational systems are legitimate, including the use of rewards and punishments.

## WCF 19.7

### *The law and the gospel*

14. Chapter 19 is one of the longer in the confession. How does the commentary summarize its different parts, and where does this section fit in?

15. Have you ever heard the claim that the law is contrary to the grace of the gospel? How would you respond? Consider Galatians 3:21 and other passages to demonstrate how the law and gospel 'sweetly comply'.

### *Spirit-enabled obedience*

16. What does it mean for the law to be written on our hearts? (See Jer. 31:33 with Heb. 8:10.) What does this teach us about the importance of the law in the new covenant?

17. What kind of obedience does the Spirit enable? How might you encourage this obedience in those under your care? Be specific, considering difficult situations.

18. Consider closing your study by praying for this kind of obedience for yourself and for those under your care.

# CHAPTER 20:

# OF CHRISTIAN LIBERTY, AND LIBERTY OF CONSCIENCE

## WCF 20.1

### *What Christ has purchased*

1. The commentary reminds us that Christian freedoms were bought at a price. How should this influence the way we use our freedom?

2. From what has Christ freed his people? Use Scripture to support your answer. What does it mean that Christ frees his people from the 'evil of afflictions'? How is that different from being delivered from affliction itself?

3. How does Scripture describe the way Jesus Christ transforms the believer's experience of death?

4. The previous questions consider what Jesus has freed us *from*. What has Jesus freed his people *to*? (See Rom. 5:1-2 and other passages.)

5. Compare a believer under the new covenant with a believer's liberty under the old. What do they have in common? What are three ways in which a Christian's liberty is enlarged under the New Testament? What do you appreciate about these enlarged freedoms? Of the many Christian freedoms discussed in this study, which one do you want to celebrate more clearly?

## WCF 20.2

### *Liberation under lordship*

6. What impact does Christ's lordship have on your conscience?

7. Are you ever tempted to become a 'slave of man'? Is there a particular person or situation that pressures you? How can you resist this pressure? (See 1 Cor. 7:23.)

8. How might you pressure others to follow you rather than God? What precautions can you take against manipulating others, or lording your position over those under your authority? (For help, see Matt. 23:8-10; 2 Cor. 1:24; Matt. 15:9; 1 Pet. 5.)

9. What reasons does the Apostle Paul give for not following the doctrines of man? Which most compels you? (For help, see Col. 2:20-23; Gal. 1:10; 2:4-5; 5:1.)

# WCF 20.3

## *Freedom within biblical bounds*

1. What is the difference between license and Christian liberty?

2. The commentary points out, 'Finding freedom from sin by serving the Lord and his people is the vision that God presents to us in his Word'. Where do we see this in the Word? Is this your vision for yourself? If so, how have you experienced this freedom already? What opportunities do you have to serve and experience this freedom more?

3. How are Christians not to use their freedom? (Gal. 5:13; 1 Pet. 2:16) What temptations do you face to use your 'freedom for the flesh'? When might there be a blurry line between using your freedom for selfish reasons and using it to serve others? What should we do when this distinction seems unclear to us?

4. Is there something in your life now, or in the past, that promises you freedom, but in the end, enslaves you? Money? Food? Success?

# WCF 20.4

## *Law and liberty*

5. What is your attitude toward lawful powers—both those in the church and those in the civil government? Do you see these lawful powers as complementary to your liberty or in tension with it? According to Scripture, what should our attitude be towards lawful powers? Why?

## *No freedom for lawlessness*

6. What responsibility does the church have to hold people accountable for practices that are against 'the light of nature'? Have you seen a church carry out such discipline well? (For help, see Rom. 1:32 with 1 Cor. 5:1, 5, 11, 13.)

7. What does Scripture tell us about different ways the church can hold people accountable? What kind of problems might warrant each response? (See 2 John 10-11 and 2 Thess. 3:14; 1 Tim. 6:3-5; Titus 1:10-11, 13 and 3:10 with Matt. 18:15-17.) How would you respond to someone who said that these measures of discipline don't carry enough weight? Support your answer with Scripture.

## *Church censures and civil magistrates*

8. How does discipline for doctrinal sin differ between the Old Testament and the New Testament? What principle undergirds this?

9. Is there a time when you have seen the church censure someone for that person's good? What makes this so difficult? What principles should we keep in mind in order to censure well? (See Rom. 13:3-4 with 2 John 10-11.)

10. What are the proper spheres of the church and the state in matters of discipline?

11. In closing, consider thanking God for his freeing us to serve him better. In light of 1 Timothy 2:2, pray also for your civil and church leaders.

# WORSHIP

—

CHAPTER 21:

# OF RELIGIOUS WORSHIP, AND THE SABBATH DAY

---

❦

**WCF 21.1**

*Worshipping by the light of nature*

1. Based on Romans 1:20, what two attributes of God does mankind know by the light of nature? What impact does this have for worship?

2. What does Scripture teach us about the character of God and how we ought to respond to him? (For help see Acts 17:24; Psa. 119:68; Mark 12:33.) Compare this with how people actually respond to God. Note a particular area in which you would like to grow.

*The acceptable way of worship*

3. In what four ways are we forbidden to worship God, as summarized by the confession?

4. What does Scripture teach us about what kinds of worship the Lord detests? Cite three or more references. What are examples of each today?

5. In light of this study, do you have any worship practices or habits that may appear wise, but upon further reflection, need to change?

## WCF 21.2-4

### *Trinitarian worship*

6. How can we make our worship specifically trinitarian? Why is this important? (Consider the apostolic blessing in 2 Cor. 13:14 as well as Matt. 4:10 with John 5:23.)

### *God alone, but not alone*

7. What does the commentator mean by the phrase, we are to worship 'God alone, but not alone'? How does Scripture support this point?

### *Prayer through Christ by the power of the Spirit*

8. How important is prayer in worship? What should characterize our prayer? (Consider Phil. 4:6.)

9. Who does God call to pray? Do you pray? Do those under your care pray? How can you help them with their praying?

10. What makes our prayers acceptable? How does this impact your prayers?

11. What are some reasons that we can have 'tremendous confidence' in prayer? (See Rom. 8:26 and 1 John 5:14.)

### *How we pray*

12. 'The manner in which we pray is also a matter of concern to the Lord', notes the commentary. What does the confession tell us about how we are to pray? Where do you see this in Scripture? What stands out as an area where you want to grow?

13. How would prayer in an unknown language be antithetical to the teaching about prayer given in this chapter?

### *For what are we to pray?*

14. Does God ask us to discern his secret will before we pray? What does Scripture tell us about this? How much freedom do we have in our prayers? (See 1 John 5:14.)

15. How does the law, including all of God's commands, help us in our prayers? Is there a command that you would like to pray for yourself?

16. For whom are we not to pray? According to the commentary what is 'the one sin that leads to death'? (See John 5:16.) How does the commentary advise us to pray?

17. For whom would you like to pray with renewed hope today?

## WCF 21.5

### *Public worship—Reading*

1. How does Scripture encourage the reading of the Word of God in both public and private worship? What practical steps can you take to better follow this direction?

### *Public worship—Preaching*

2. What does 2 Timothy 4:2 tell us about the practice of preaching? How would you define the confession's term, 'sound preaching'? What do you consider the most important quality of preaching when either listening to or delivering a sermon? What competes with this priority?

### *Public worship—Hearing*

3. What does the term 'conscionable' mean as it describes how we hear preaching? What examples and counter examples of such hearing do we find in Scripture? Which area would you like to grow in as a hearer?

### *Public worship—Singing*

4. What does the confession mean by stating that we are to sing 'psalms with grace in the heart'? (For help see Col. 3:16; Eph. 5:19; James 5:13.) How can you better put your heart into your singing? How can you help those under your care to do so as well?

## Public worship—Sacraments

5. What does Scripture teach us about how and why we should receive the sacraments? How does the confession express this?

## Private worship

6. What biblical examples do we see of oaths, vows, fasting, and thanksgiving as worship? In what ways should these be incorporated into our worship, whether it be public or private?

7. What words in this section highlight our attitude in worship? Where does your worship fall short? Will you confess this to God? How would you like to pray for your worship to grow in maturity?

## WCF 21.6

## No place for prayer?

8. How does the commentary address the matter of 'sacred' spaces for worship under the gospel? How does Scripture speak to this? How is this liberating? How is the idea of sacred space popular today? What is the appeal and what is the danger?

## Prayer in every place, and on all occasions

9. Who does God call to pray? When and where does God call people to pray? What does God threaten to all who do not pray? (See Job 10:25.)

10. What does God require of our worship in John 4:23-24? How does this relate to the Trinity?

## Family worship

11. What does the confession say about family worship? Can you speak of ways family worship has helped your family spiritually? How does Scripture commend family worship?

12. The commentary suggests that the Lord's Prayer is particularly useful for families. What are its benefits? How can one incorporate it in family prayers?

## Personal and public worship

13. How do we know that we are to worship God privately? What does our private worship say about our faith?

14. How does Scripture present public prayer and worship as essential parts of the life of God's people? (See Isa. 56:6-7; Heb. 10:25; Prov. 1:20-21, 24; 8:34.)

15. Reflecting on God's requirement that all people worship, is there someone you would like to invite to church? Consider praying for the opportunity and boldness to invite and that this person would accept your invitation. Consider also praying for a specific way you can grow in your worship, be it public or private.

❧

**WCF 21.7**

*A law of nature, a perpetual commandment*

1. What promise comes from keeping one day in seven holy to the Lord? (Consider Exod. 20:8, 10-11 and Isa. 56:2, 4, 6- 7.)

*For clarification: Sabbaths and the Sabbath*

2. What is the difference between what the commentary calls 'Sabbaths' and 'the Sabbath'? From Leviticus 23, what are some examples of first-day Sabbaths? What distinguished them from the last-day Sabbath introduced in Genesis 2:2-3?

*The last is now first*

3. In the New Testament era after Christ's resurrection, the Sabbath was changed from the last day of the week to the first. How does the commentary present Christ as a fulfilment of the Old Testament feasts celebrated on the first day?

4. When did Paul expect Christians to meet regularly? How do we know?

5. Why is it fitting that we call this new Sabbath 'The Lord's day'?

6. Why is this day of rest 'to be continued to the end of the world, as the Christian Sabbath'? Use Scripture to support your answer.

## WCF 21.8

### *Keeping a day holy*

7. What does the moral law command us to do in regard to the Christian Sabbath?

8. What examples do we see of people planning ahead for the Sabbath in the Old Testament? How can Sabbath preparation enable us to enjoy greater rest on the Sabbath? What are various kinds of preparations you could make, in mind, body, home and work? With these preparations, what Sabbath blessings do you anticipate?

9. How does Scripture tie work and rest together? How is this a model for us? (See Exod. 20:8-11; 31:15-17.)

10. How did keeping the Sabbath require faith from Old Testament believers? How does it require faith from you? (See Exod. 16:23, 25-26, 29-30.)

### *The character of the day*

11. What does Scripture tell us about the intended character of the Sabbath Day?

12. The commentary warns against being 'over-prescriptive in defining the structures and activities' of the Sabbath. What does the commentary suggest as some basic principles to keep in mind?

13. How has this study impacted your understanding of the Sabbath? Are there any changes you want to make? Consider closing your study in prayer, giving thanks for the

blessing of the Sabbath and praying for the wisdom we need to honour it this week and onwards until the final Sabbath rest.

# CHAPTER 22:

# OF LAWFUL OATHS AND VOWS

---

❦

## WCF 22.1-2

### *The good kind of swearing*

1. Why is a lawful oath rightly understood to be an act of worship?

2. Based on biblical examples, can you name any kinds of legitimate swearing which we can and should do today? How might taking a lawful oath, imposed by a lawful authority, glorify God?

### *In God's name*

3. How does Scripture warn us regarding oaths and vows? Can you describe a situation when you especially need to remember these warnings?

## WCF 22.3-4

### *Speaking the truth and swearing to do good*

4. How would you describe Old Testament examples and warnings against avoiding good oaths? (See Num. 5:19, 21; Exod. 22:7-11; Neh. 5:12.)

### *No equivocation*

5. Why do we need oaths?

6. Have you been tempted to break your word based on who it was given to?

## WCF 22.5-7

### *Fulfil what you vow / Vows are to the Lord*

7. Based on the confession's use of the terms, how are vows and oaths alike and how are they different? Based on biblical examples, what are some characteristics of vows?

8. What warnings does Scripture give against unfulfilled vows? On the flip side, why might a vow be useful?

9. In light of our human limitations what are some useful phrases to put in a vow?

### *Foolish vows*

10. What kind of vows ought we to avoid? How might you be tempted at work or school to make more promises than you ought?

11. How does reflecting on vows and oaths help you to better appreciate the promises that God makes to you? What is one particular promise of God that you would like to revel in today?

12. In closing your study on oaths and vows, how would you like to praise God? How would you like to pray for yourself and those under your care?

# CIVIL GOVERNMENT
# AND FAMILY

———

# CHAPTER 23:

# OF THE CIVIL MAGISTRATE

‧

## WCF 23.1-2

*The Lord of the lords, and King of the kings*

1. How does this chapter open? Why is this important?

2. What does the term 'civil magistrate' encompass? (See 1 Pet. 2:13-14.)

## The sword

3. What is 'the sword'? From where do civil magistrates get this power? (See Rom. 13:4.) What impact should this have on our obedience to them?

4. What is the twofold purpose for civil magistrates? Why is this important to keep in mind?

### Christian magistrates

5. Describe three misunderstandings of how Christians should relate to the government, as presented in the commentary. What is the biblical alternative?

6. How does Scripture imply an approval of believers taking an office in the government? How does the confession summarize the responsibilities of Christian magistrates?

7. How does Scripture instruct us to pray for magistrates?

### Just war

8. What does the confession say about war? How does Scripture support this?

## WCF 23.3

### Limits to authority

9. How does the Old Testament draw a line between spiritual and civil service? How does the New Testament uphold this line?

### The magistrate as promoter of the church?

10. How is the line between spiritual and civil service sometimes blurred? When, in practice, does one government sometimes cross into the other's domain? Or, how does the church sometimes act like the state and the state sometimes like the church?

11. Should the civil government be 'the promoter' of the church, defending and promoting the gospel? Why did the

Westminster divines conclude that the civil government does have this duty? What Scripture did they rely upon? In contrast, why did the eighteenth-century American Presbyterian church conclude that the civil government does not have this duty to promote the church? To what Scripture did they turn?

### *The magistrate as a guide to the church?*

12. Does a civil government have the power to call synods or councils and govern those councils? Why did the seventeenth-century divines think so? Why do many Christians today believe the civil government does not have the power to call church synods or councils? What biblical principles and passages lie behind this view?

13. Broadly speaking, how should the state 'protect' the church? More specifically, what freedom of the church should the state protect? Do you believe that the state has a duty to protect all religions? Support your answers with Scripture as you are able.

## WCF 23.4

### *The duties of subjects*

14. What are the duties of subjects, according to the confession and Scripture?

15. What does the confession warn against by the phrase, 'for conscience sake'? (Consider Rom. 13:5 and Titus 3:1.) Is there a particular duty that you need to pay attention to? What are practical helps in carrying out these duties?

### *Unbelieving leaders/ Ministers of religion and the government of the state*

16. In light of 1 Peter 2:13-14, 16, what should our attitude be towards an unbelieving civil leader or human institution? Can you give an example of a situation when this attitude is difficult, yet nevertheless commanded by God's Word? What is the greater spiritual context that we ought to keep in mind as we consider our attitude toward ministers of religion and the government of the state?

17. The confession states that ecclesiastical persons are not exempt from duties to governing authorities. How does Scripture support this point?

18. How are the duties above consistent with your understanding of the gospel?

19. Has the study of the relationship between church and state authorities helped you? If so, how?

20. How would you like to give thanks for and pray for your civil magistrate? (Consider 1 Tim. 2:2 and Psa. 82:3-4.) How would you like to pray for yourself as a subject?

# CHAPTER 24:

# OF MARRIAGE, AND DIVORCE

🌿

**WCF 24.1-3**

*Defining marriage: one man and one woman*

1. What pattern of marriage does God establish at creation? (See Gen. 2:24.) How does wisdom from the book of Proverbs and Jesus' teaching reinforce the Genesis pattern? (See Prov. 2:17 and Matt. 19:5-6.)

2. How does this statement speak into gender and marriage confusion today?

*What is the purpose of marriage?*

3. What is the fourfold purpose of marriage? How does Scripture support each purpose? How does divorce undermine these purposes?

*Whom should Christians marry?*

4. How does the New Testament affirm that marriage is not only for Christians? What does the commentator mean by saying that Christians should be 'marriage maximalists'?

*Marrying in the Lord*

5. What is the chief boundary in this choice? Use Scripture to support your answer.

6. What problems can come from a believer marrying an unbeliever? What are some scriptural examples of the grief such marriages have brought?

## WCF 24.4-6

### Consanguinity or affinity

7. What additional limit does the confession point out regarding the person whom one can marry? How does the commentary support this using Scripture?

8. How is marital engagement affected by pre-marital sexual relations? (Matt. 1:18-20.) What does this say about the value of sexual purity?

9. How does the confession's teaching on divorce compare with common practice today? What do you believe is right and why?

10. Why ought there be a public and orderly proceeding in the case of divorce? (Consider Deut. 24:1-4.)

11. In closing this study, consider thanking God for the institution of marriage. How would you like to pray for those considering marriage? For those in a difficult marriage? For your government's protection of marriage? How would you like to pray for yourself?

# THE CHURCH

# CHAPTER 25:

# OF THE CHURCH

❧

## WCF 25.1

### An 'invisible' church

1. What is the invisible church and why is that term used? (Consider Eph. 1:10, 5:27, 32.)

### The head of the church

2. What images does Scripture use to describe the relation between Christ and the church? What do these images teach us?

### The fullness of Christ

3. As a description of the church, what does 'the fullness of him that fills all in all' mean—and what does it not? How does this speak to the importance of the church?

## WCF 25.2

### Universal and visible

4. How do we know from Scripture that the church is not confined to one nation? What are some practical implications of this?

### Professors and 'their children'

5. What emphasis does the confession give to public profession of faith and why?

6. How does Scripture describe children of believers as set apart from the world for God? What are some ways that the Old Testament includes children as God's people? How does the Apostle Peter's preaching affirm this inclusion? How do you?

### The church as kingdom, house, and family

7. What privileges and responsibilities are implied by Scripture's referring to the church as the family of God? (See Eph. 2:19; 3:15.) How have you experienced these privileges and responsibilities?

### Inside and outside the church

8. In the New Testament, how does devotion to Christ relate to commitment to the church? (See Acts 2:47 and other passages that come to mind.) What does commitment to the church look like in your life?

## WCF 25.3

### *The ministry, oracles, and ordinances*

9. The commentary asks 'To whom does the ministry belong?' How does the Apostle Paul's teaching about gifts give us insight into this question? (See 1 Cor. 12:28.) What implications does this have?

### *Gathering and perfecting*

10. How does Scripture express the twofold purpose of the church? Do you tend to think of the church as serving one purpose more than the other? How can we keep both in view?

### *To the end of the world*

11. What promises does Christ give to encourage the church in her task?

12. How do these promises impact you and your participation at church?

❧

## WCF 25.4-6

### *The visibility of the church, and the marks of the church*

1. What does the confession mean by saying that 'this catholic church has been sometimes more, sometimes less visible'?

(Consider Rom. 11:3-4 and Rev. 12:6, 14.) In your experience, how visible has the church been?

2. According to what three marks does paragraph 4 evaluate the purity of the church?

3. What are your priorities when looking for a home church? Support your answer with reasons from Scripture.

### Mixed churches

4. Why do we all need to graciously accept our church as less than ideal? What does this acceptance look like? (Consider 1 Cor. 13:12 and Matt. 13:24-30.)

5. How would you distinguish a church 'subject to mixture, and error' from what the confession calls a 'synagogue of Satan'? (For help see Rev. 18:2 and Rom. 11:18-22.)

6. Although the church is vulnerable to becoming 'less visible', how does Scripture give the church strength and comfort? How should these promises affect your commitment to the church? When might we especially need to hear these promises?

### The only head of the church

7. How does Scripture describe Christ's headship over the church?

8. The commentary instructs church leaders: 'we should never set ourselves up as people who must be obeyed—our authority is merely derivative and representative'. Practically speaking, what are some ways that leaders can show

the true nature of their authority? What are some errors to avoid? (Consider 1 Pet. 5:2-4.)

### *The pope as the antichrist?*

9. How could church members give too much authority to a church leader? (Consider Matt. 23:8-10.) How is the church today at risk of treating someone other than Christ as head of the church?

10. In light of the Scripture's teaching on the church, consider giving thanks for the church and God's promises to her. How would you like to pray for your church and its leaders? How would you like to pray for yourself and those under your care?

CHAPTER 26:

# OF THE COMMUNION
# OF SAINTS

❦

## WCF 26.1

### Union with Christ

1. What is the shift in focus from Chapter 25 to Chapter 26? How does the commentary summarize the three sections of this chapter?

2. What experiences do believers share with Christ because of their union with him? (Consider a broad range and support your answer with Scripture.) How do you relate to these experiences? Which in particular stand out to you?

### Communion with the saints

3. How can the communion of the saints contribute to a Christian's growth? Cite Scripture in your answer.

4. Paragraph 1 states that all saints have 'communion in each other's gifts and graces'. What are some specific ways you experienced such communion recently—either by serving or receiving?

5. What obligations do Christians have towards one another, as summarized by 1 Thessalonians 5:11-14? How do you see Christians carrying out this obligation in families? In churches? Is there a particular area in which you would like to grow?

**WCF 26.2-3**

*The worship of God*

6. How is the early church described in Acts 2:42-46? Is there a specific way you want to better follow its example?

7. How do you see the prophecy in Isaiah 2:3 fulfilled in the New Testament church? How can this prophecy be an encouragement to you today?

8. What warning and command do you find in Hebrews 10:24-25? How are they particularly relevant to the church today? Do you face any temptations to neglect corporate worship for something else—if so, what? Why is meeting together so important?

9. Paragraph 2 says that 'mutual edification' should be our goal. How does Scripture support this? What opportunities do you have to edify someone else at church? These may be direct (such as teaching a class or having a caring

conversation), or indirect (such as serving in the nursery so another person can attend worship).

### The 'outward things'

10. How does Scripture demonstrate the importance of carrying one another's burdens? How might God be calling you to share locally? Globally? Do you have needs that you think you should make known to the broader church so that others might share your burden?

### Qualifiers about communion: no possibility of divinization

11. The confession points out that communion with Christ does not mean becoming the same substance as him, or being equal to him. How does Scripture make it clear that Christ remains unique and superior? Cite at least three passages.

### Qualifiers about communion: no requirement for communalism

12. How does Scripture indicate that God-honouring communion between the saints still allows for private property?

13. The commentary closes this chapter with a call to be heavenly minded. How can this focus help us to share?

14. Reflecting on your study of the communion of the saints, how would you like to pray for yourself and others?

CHAPTER 27:

# OF THE SACRAMENTS

———————

❦

## WCF 27.1-2

### *Signs and seals of the covenant of grace*

1. How are sacraments 'signs and seals'? Consider the meaning of these terms during the time the Westminster Confession was written. How does this meaning reflect the language of Scripture? (See Rom. 4:11.)

### *Given by God*

2. How can we see in Scripture that the sacraments were instituted by God and not by man? What difference does this make regarding the way that you receive the sacraments?

### *Four functions of sacraments*

3. What four purposes do the sacraments serve according to the confession? How does Scripture support each purpose?

## Sacramental union

4. When the Bible speaks about the sacraments and salvation, how, on occasion, are 'the names and effects of the one attributed to the other'? (For help, see Gen. 17:10; Matt. 26:27-28 and Titus 3:5.) Why is this important to understand?

## WCF 27.3-5

### Grace exhibited

5. On what (or on whom) does the effectiveness of the sacraments depend? On what (or on whom) does it not? Use Scripture to support your answer.

6. Why do words of institution and teaching accompany the sacraments? Where do we see this in Scripture?

### A minister

7. What does the confession say about who is eligible to administer the sacraments? How does this mirror the teaching of Scripture?

### Two sacraments

8. What are a few reasons why we only celebrate two sacraments?

### In the substance the same

9. Why could Paul refer to the Exodus as a baptism? (See 1 Cor. 10:1-4.)

10. How has your understanding of the sacraments been deepened through this study? Consider thanking God in prayer for the sacraments and your understanding of them.

CHAPTER 28:

# OF BAPTISM

⸻

🌿

## WCF 28.1

*The baptism of the Christian church*

1. Give one or more reasons why baptism is important (as discussed in the commentary and seen in Scripture).

*A five-fold spiritual significance*

2. What is the five-fold spiritual significance of baptism and how do we see this in Scripture?

3. What does the commentary identify as the primary and secondary reference of baptism? How is this distinction helpful?

## WCF 28.2-3

*Water*

4. How does Scripture support that water alone is to be used in baptism? (See Matt. 3:11 and John 1:33.)

5. What does Matthew 28:19-20 teach us about the persons who ought to administer baptism and into whose name it is administered? If a minister is not faithful, is a baptism done by him in the name of the triune God still valid? Why, or why not?

### Dipping, pouring, and sprinkling

6. What are four cases in Scripture where baptismal washing is symbolic, involving little water? Where else does the action of sprinkling or pouring symbolize the divine work of salvation? (Consider Heb. 10:22 for a start.)

7. How might one respond to the view that immersion is necessary to picture burial? (For help, see Rom. 6 and Col. 2.)

## WCF 28.4

### Baptizing believers

8. What are some of the important elements in the baptisms we see in Scripture (Acts 2:41; 8:12-13; 16:14-15)? Considering both what is explicit and what is implied, what do these baptisms have in common?

9. If we base our theology on explicit proof texts only and not theological reasoning, how would we limit our view of baptism?

### Covenantal continuity

10. What are some examples of covenantal continuity between the Old Testament and the New Testament?

11. What is the parallel between circumcision and baptism in Colossians 2:11-12? Why is this significant? What are some implications for God's people?

### *Baptizing infants*

12. How many believing parents does a child require in order to be considered set apart to the Lord? What does this tell us about God's character? (See 1 Cor. 7:14.)

13. Are there ways in which baptism is more inclusive than circumcision? (Consider Matt. 28:19.) How would restricting children from receiving the sign of the covenant diverge from the general expansion of the new covenant?

14. What is Jesus' attitude toward children? Show from Scripture. How does infant baptism reflect this attitude?

15. What prayer does the commentary suggest for parents giving their children the sign and seal of the gospel? Consider praying this for children you know.

❧

## WCF 28.5-7

### *Neglecting baptism*

1. What danger is there in rejecting the sign of the covenant? Use Scripture to support your answer.

*An inseparable annex?*

2. Can one be regenerated, or saved, without receiving the sign of the promise? Why, or why not?

*Baptismal regeneration?*

3. What does the example of Simon Magus teach us about the relationship between baptism and regeneration? (Consider Acts 8:13, 23.)

*When is baptism useful?*

4. WCF 28.5 and the commentary point out that the usefulness of baptism is not tied to the moment of time when administered. Then when is baptism useful? (Consider parallels to regeneration as described in John 3:5-8.)

5. How does Scripture point to the effectiveness of baptism in conveying God's grace?

6. If a friend were thinking of being re-baptized and asked you for advice, what might you say? What questions might you ask? What Scriptures might you highlight? What theological principles might you use?

7. As you close your study on baptism, consider thanking God for this sacrament and the gospel to which it points. Consider also praying that we would understand and appreciate baptism more, for our own good and for the good of others.

CHAPTER 29:

# OF THE LORD'S SUPPER

———————

🌿

**WCF 29.1**

*The sacrament of body and blood*

1. Paragraph 1 highlights that the Lord Jesus instituted the Lord's supper on the night wherein he was betrayed. How is it useful to remember the original setting of the supper?

2. The commentary identifies nine 'cardinal truths' about the supper and what it represents. What are they? How does Scripture support each truth? Why is each important? Which truth do you want to reflect upon and why?

**WCF 29.2**

*Not an offering, not a sacrifice*

3. How does paragraph 2 relate to paragraph 1?

4. What three aspects of Roman Catholic doctrine is paragraph 2 refuting? How do Hebrews 9:22 and 9:25-26 support the confession here?

### *A commemorative offering or a commemoration of an offering?*

5. The commentary describes the supper as a 'commemoration of an offering' in contrast to a 'commemorative offering'. How would you explain the difference between the two? (Consider 1 Cor. 11:24-26 and Matt. 26:26-27.)

6. How is the Catholic mass inconsistent with Hebrews 7:23-24 and 7:27?

7. What does Jesus' position at the right hand of God tell us about Christ's sacrifice? (See Heb. 10:11-14.)

8. How does Hebrews 10:18 confirm the effectiveness of Christ's sacrifice in atoning for sin?

9. If someone were to say to you that the Roman Catholic church is not that much different from your own, how might you respond? How important is this sacrament in understanding that difference?

## WCF 29.3-4

### *Celebrating the supper*

10. How do the third and fourth paragraphs connect to the first two?

11. What are three key features of the Lord's supper? Where do we see these features in Scripture?

### Private communion

12. What are three reasons why the Lord's supper should not be celebrated privately? Support with Scripture.

13. Are there people in your church who cannot attend corporate worship due to physical limitations? How might your church serve them?

### Pretended religion

14. What does Scripture tell us about who should drink the cup and who should not? How does this compare with historic Roman Catholic practice? (See Mark 14:23 and 1 Cor. 11:25-29.)

15. The confession warns against worshipping the elements themselves as that would be contrary to God's commands (Matt. 15:9). Is there a way that the church is particularly tempted to such error today? What practical steps might we take to help prevent this error?

## WCF 29.5-6

### *A reader's guide to the sacraments*

1. What does Jesus call the bread and the wine when he instituted the Lord's supper? What indication do you have that Jesus considered the bread and wine to remain as bread and wine? (See Matt. 26:26-29.)

2. How does Paul's language in 1 Corinthians 11:26-28 imply 'that even after these common elements are properly set apart for holy use, "they still remain truly and only bread and wine, as they were before"'.

### *The trouble with transubstantiation*

3. How is transubstantiation repugnant to Scripture? Cite references. How is transubstantiation repugnant to common sense?

4. What practical steps can be taken to avoid superstition about the supper?

## WCF 29.7-8

### *The spiritual presence of Christ in the supper*

5. How is the Lord's supper more than a mere memorial moment to remember? (Consider 1 Cor. 11:28 and 1 Cor. 10:16.)

6. What does the confession mean by stating that Christ is present 'really but spiritually' in the supper? What is the purpose of this distinction?

*Eating and drinking damnation*

7. What does Scripture tell us about the harm done when someone takes the supper without faith or understanding?

8. When a minister warns a congregation about taking the supper, who is the warning meant to keep away and who not? Support your answer with Scripture.

9. How does the confession's teaching impact your understanding of the Lord's supper? How does it affect how you partake of the Lord's supper? How would you like to pray in light of your study?

# CHAPTER 30:

# OF CHURCH CENSURES

❧

## WCF 30.1-2

### *The government of the church*

1. How does Scripture support the confession's statement that Jesus is 'the king and head of the church' with 'all authority in heaven and on earth'? Cite references.

2. What are some scriptural terms for church officers?

3. How does Scripture describe the duties of church officers? Cite references.

4. In one word, how could you summarize the relationship between ecclesiastical and civil governments?

### *The keys of the kingdom*

5. Where does the expression 'keys of the kingdom' come from and what does it mean?

6. Did Jesus presume some kind of church membership? Why do you think so?

7. Since 'the sword' belongs to civil authorities alone, by what means do church officers execute their duties? (Consider John 20:23 and 2 Cor. 2:6-8.) What does this look like in practice?

8. Do you recognize ways the church sometimes neglects to use her power? On the flip side, can you recognize ways the church sometimes oversteps her bounds and uses 'the sword'?

9. Why is it important for a believer to join a church? How does a good use of church membership convey gospel encouragement and warnings?

## WCF 30.3-4

### *What are church censures for?*

10. What are five reasons why church discipline is necessary? How does Scripture support these reasons?

### *Degrees of discipline*

11. What are some examples of different methods and degrees of censure that officers may choose to use? Cite Scripture to support your answer.

12. What are the benefits of church censure being carried out by church officers rather than by a congregation?

13. After your study on church censures, how would you like to pray for your elders? For yourself? For those under your care? How would you like to thank God for church discipline?

# OF SYNODS AND COUNCILS

❦

## WCF 31.1; 31.2 / RCF 31.1

*A case for councils*

1. How does Chapter 31 build on Chapter 30?

2. Why is it important to note that even while the apostles were active, they chose to call a gathering of elders to settle their disputes rather than employ their apostolic authority only? What does this teach us about church authority?

*Who can call a synod? Historic British and American perspectives*

3. What are some differences you see between the Westminster Assembly's first paragraph in Chapter 31 and the American revisions in paragraphs 1 and 2? (The commentary notes seven.)

4. What does the commentary mean by noting 'the church, as the New Israel, is more analogous to Israel in exile than

Israel in Canaan'? As convenient as it might seem, what are some reasons why a church should not be led by a political entity? (Consider 1 Pet. 1:1 and Acts 15:2-4, 22-23.)

## WCF 31.3 / RCF 31.2

### *The threefold task of synods and councils*

5. What are three tasks of synods and councils? How do we see this in the early church?

6. Does your church use synods or councils? Can you give an example of how they are working on one or more of these tasks?

### *Ministerial* and *authoritative*

7. How are decisions of councils to be received? How do we know this is true for councils today and not just during the time of the apostles? (Consider Acts 15:28 and Acts 16:4.)

8. The commentary suggests, 'the Word of God itself is calling us to heed councils not less, but more'. How might a church benefit from councils more?

## WCF 31.4-5 / RCF 31.3-4

### *A doctrinal declaration*

9. How were the apostles and their teaching unique and different from all synods and councils that followed? (Consider Eph. 2:20.) What claims to the contrary does the church face today?

### *An historical observation*

10. In the history of the church, what are some examples of errors of councils?

### *Biblical directives*

11. How might the church today sometimes err, making the word of councils the guide above Scripture? (For help, see Acts 17:11; 1 Cor. 2:5; 2 Cor. 1:24.) How does the confession's teaching on councils cohere with its teaching on Holy Scripture in Chapter 1?

### *Synods, councils, and civil affairs*

12. How do Jesus' own words support a limited view of church power and authority?

### *Petitions and advice*

13. What two exceptions does the assembly offer to the general rule against meddling in civil affairs? What Scripture supports this?

14. How can you express your views to the civil government in a humble manner? Is there a way that you, either on your own or with a group, are doing this?

15. Given your present civil government, can you imagine a situation where it would be difficult to give an answer for what you believe? What would you like to say?

16. In light of this study, how would you like to pray for yourself, for your church, and for church councils?

# THE LAST THINGS

Chapter 32: Of the State of Men after Death,
and of the Resurrection of the Dead
(One Study)

Chapter 33: Of the Last Judgment
(One Study)

CHAPTER 32:

# OF THE STATE OF MEN AFTER DEATH, AND OF THE RESURRECTION OF THE DEAD

❦

**WCF 32.1**

*Dust to dust*

1. What are some passages that help us face the reality of our own death—unless the Lord should return first? How can facing this reality help you in life?

*Immortal subsistence*

2. When a person dies, where does the body and where does the spirit go? Cite Scripture to support your answer.

*Waiting for redemption*

3. What reasons do Christians have to feel peace and courage in the face of death? Cite Scripture to support your answer.

## Reserved for judgment

4. By contrast, what reasons do non-Christians have to feel terror in the face of death? Support your answer with Scripture.

5. What danger can you see in thinking there is a place beside heaven or hell where souls go?

## WCF 32.2-3

### Never to die

6. What will happen to believers who are still alive at Christ's return? (See 1 Thess. 4:17.)

7. What can we be certain about for all believers at the day of Christ's return, whether alive or dead? How can this thought help you to persevere in godliness today?

### Ever to live

8. What will the raised body of the believer be like? Support your answer with Scripture.

### Dishonour and honour

9. In reference to the resurrection, what does the commentary call 'the horror of this reality'? How does Scripture contrast the resurrection of believers with that of unbelievers?

10. While Scripture reveals some things about the resurrection body, what aspect of the resurrection body still remains a mystery to us? What should our response be toward that

which we know and that which we do not know? (Consider 1 Cor. 15:51.)

11. How would you like to give thanks today for the promised resurrection at the last day?

# CHAPTER 33

# OF THE LAST JUDGMENT

## WCF 33.1

### *The Judge*

1. How does Scripture emphasize the certainty of the coming judgment?

### *Angels*

2. What warnings and encouragement can we find from the judgment of angels? Support your answer with Scripture.

### *Human beings*

3. How does Scripture describe the extent of the judgment on humanity?

4. What warning do you take from Scripture's teaching about the coming judgment?

5. In the face of judgment, where do you find courage?

6. How does your study on the coming judgment impact your present way of life?

## WCF 33.2

### *The purposes of God's judgment*

7. According to the confession, what is the twofold purpose of God's judgment?

8. What does the commentary call 'the most surprising aspect' to Jesus' account of judgment day? (See Matt. 25:31-46.)

### *God, not man*

9. Who will be the focus on judgment day? How do you feel about that?

10. What attributes of God will be glorified at the judgment? (See Rom. 9:22-23; Matt. 26:21; Rom. 2:5-6; 2 Thess. 1:7-10.) On which of these attributes do you want to reflect for your encouragement today?

11. Given 'the glory of the eternal state for believers, and the horror of the eternal state for the lost', with whom do you want to share the urgent message of the gospel? Consider praying for your witness to this person (or these people), and that his or her response would follow the command of Acts 3:19.

# WCF 33.3

## *A certain day*

12. Has the certainty of the coming judgment deterred you from sin? How might it more?

13. The confession states that we need to be persuaded of the coming judgment. How does Scripture emphasize this as a need? How might this impact your witness to the gospel?

14. How does keeping the return of Christ in mind console you in adversity? Can you offer examples from your life?

15. What two attitudes should we have toward the coming judgment? (See Rom 8:23-25.) Consider what this might look like in day-to-day life, including any way you would like to grow.

## *An unknown date*

16. What is a major purpose of God's leaving the date of judgment day unknown to men? Support your answer with Scripture.

17. What can you do to welcome the Lord's return? (Consider Rev. 22:20.) In light of this, how might you pray for yourself and others?

The Banner of Truth Trust originated in 1957 in London. The founders believed that much of the best literature of historic Christianity had been allowed to fall into oblivion and that, under God, its recovery could well lead not only to a strengthening of the church, but to true revival.

Inter-denominational in vision, this publishing work is now international, and our lists include a number of contemporary authors along with classics from the past. The translation of these books into many languages is encouraged.

A monthly magazine, *The Banner of Truth*, is also published. More information about this and all our publications can be found on our website or supplied by either of the offices below.

## THE BANNER OF TRUTH TRUST

3 Murrayfield Road
Edinburgh, EH12 6EL
UK

PO Box 621, Carlisle,
Pennsylvania 17013,
USA

www.banneroftruth.org